This **BASICS** book
belongs to

SCOTT

USA

The World

The Galaxy

The Universe

First Aladdin Books edition 1991

First published in 1990 by David Bennett Books Limited
94 Victoria Street, St Albans, Herts AL1 3TG, England

Series Editor: Ruth Thomson
Consultants: Professor W. M. Blaney, Department of Biology,
Birkbeck College, University of London, and
The Natural History Museum, London, and
Samuel Taylor, Ph.D., Biology Director,
The New York Hall of Science, New York

Aladdin Books
Macmillan Publishing Company
866 Third Avenue
New York, NY 10022

Printed in Hong Kong

1 2 3 4 5 6 7 8 9 10

Library of Congress Cataloging–in–Publication Data
Thomson, Ruth
Creepy Crawlies / written by Ruth Thomson: illustrated by Dom
Mansell.—1st Aladdin Books ed.
p. cm.—(Aladdin basics)
Includes index.
Summary: An introduction to such"creepy crawlies" as ants,
caterpillars, flies, snails, spiders, and worms.
ISBN 0–689–71489–0
1. Insects—Juvenile literature. 2. Arthropoda—Juvenile
literature. [1. Insects. 2. Arthropods.] I. Mansell, Dom, ill.
II. Title. III. Series.
QL467.2T48 1991
592—dc20 91–7482 CIP AC

**Don't worry! We have drawn most of the creepy crawlies
in this book much larger than they are in real life.
This is so you can see what they really look like.**

Creepy Crawlies

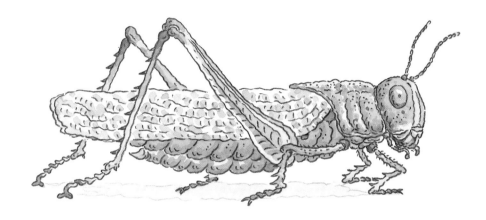

Written by
Ruth Thomson

Illustrated by
Dom Mansell

Aladdin Books
Macmillan Publishing Company
New York

Maxwell Macmillan International Publishing Group
New York   Oxford   Singapore   Sydney

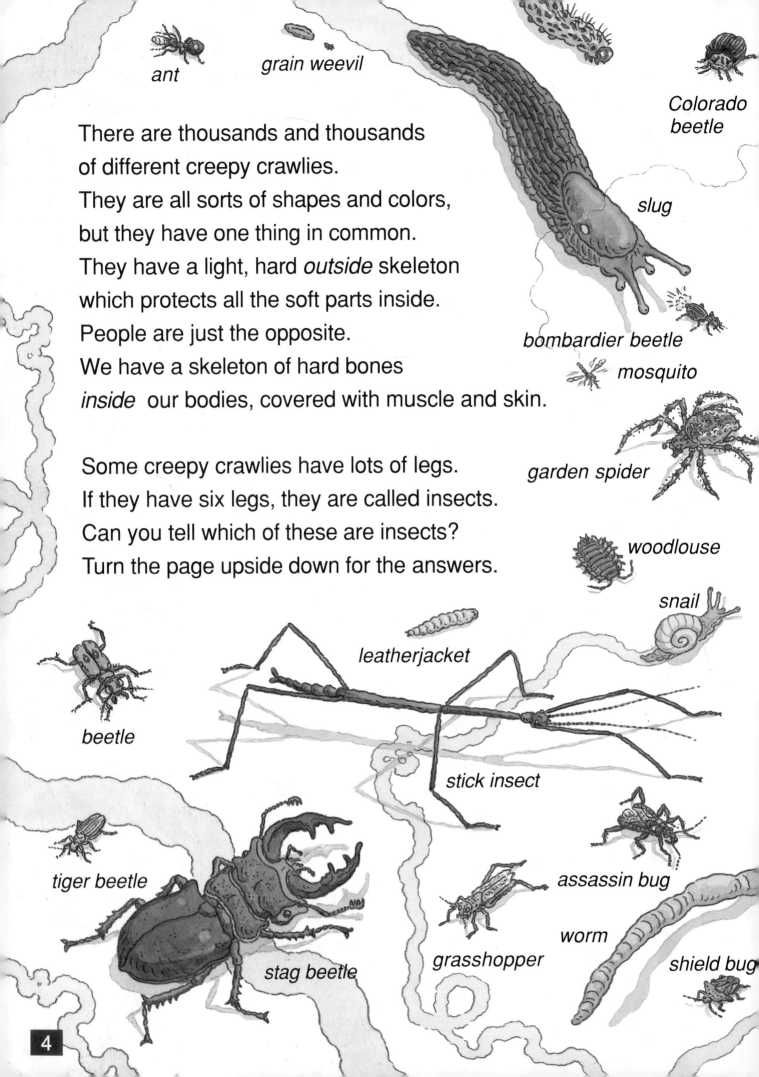

ant

grain weevil

Colorado beetle

slug

There are thousands and thousands
of different creepy crawlies.
They are all sorts of shapes and colors,
but they have one thing in common.
They have a light, hard *outside* skeleton
which protects all the soft parts inside.
People are just the opposite.
We have a skeleton of hard bones
inside our bodies, covered with muscle and skin.

Some creepy crawlies have lots of legs.
If they have six legs, they are called insects.
Can you tell which of these are insects?
Turn the page upside down for the answers.

bombardier beetle

mosquito

garden spider

woodlouse

snail

leatherjacket

beetle

stick insect

tiger beetle

assassin bug

worm

grasshopper

stag beetle

shield bug

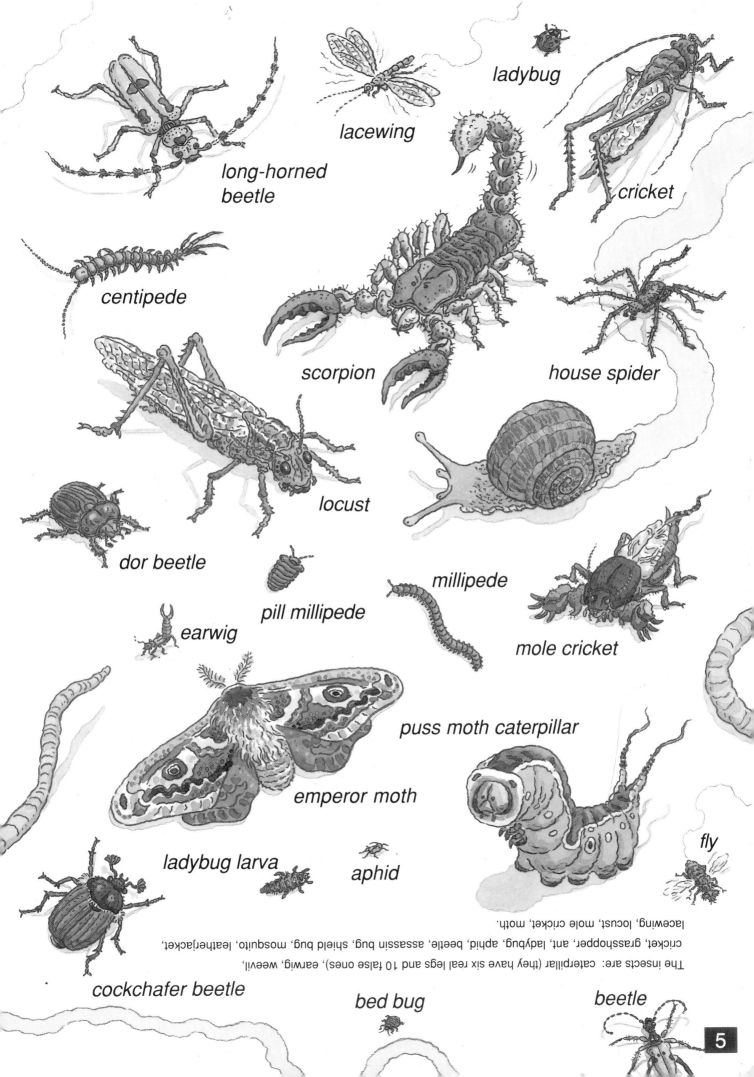

long-horned beetle

lacewing

ladybug

cricket

centipede

scorpion

house spider

locust

dor beetle

pill millipede

earwig

millipede

mole cricket

puss moth caterpillar

emperor moth

fly

ladybug larva

aphid

cockchafer beetle

bed bug

beetle

The insects are: caterpillar (they have six real legs and 10 false ones), earwig, weevil,
cricket, grasshopper, ant, ladybug, aphid, beetle, shield bug, assassin bug, mosquito, leatherjacket,
lacewing, locust, mole cricket, moth.

5

Slugs and snails have soft, slimy bodies
and no legs at all. Most live in damp places,
because their skin dries out in the sun.
They come out at night or on rainy days.

Both slugs and snails
feed on plants, especially
rotting ones. Their rows
of teeny, tiny teeth grate
and shred their food.

If a slug is frightened,
it scrunches up
into a lump.

In hot, dry weather,
the snail pulls
its whole body
into its shell.
It seals the opening,
so that it does
not dry out.

Slugs and snails have eyes
on long stalks. If they are
disturbed, they pull their eyes in.

Slugs and snails move slowly.
Their wide, muscular foot
ripples and pushes them forward.
They make a layer of sticky
slime under their foot.
This helps them to move
easily over rough surfaces.

If the tail of a worm is cut off,
it can grow back again.

Sometimes worms pull
dead leaves into
their burrows to eat.

Worms eat soil
as they tunnel underground.
Sometimes you will see little heaps
of fine soil on the ground.
These have been left by worms.
They are called worm-casts.

Worms have
wriggly bodies.
They live mainly
underground.

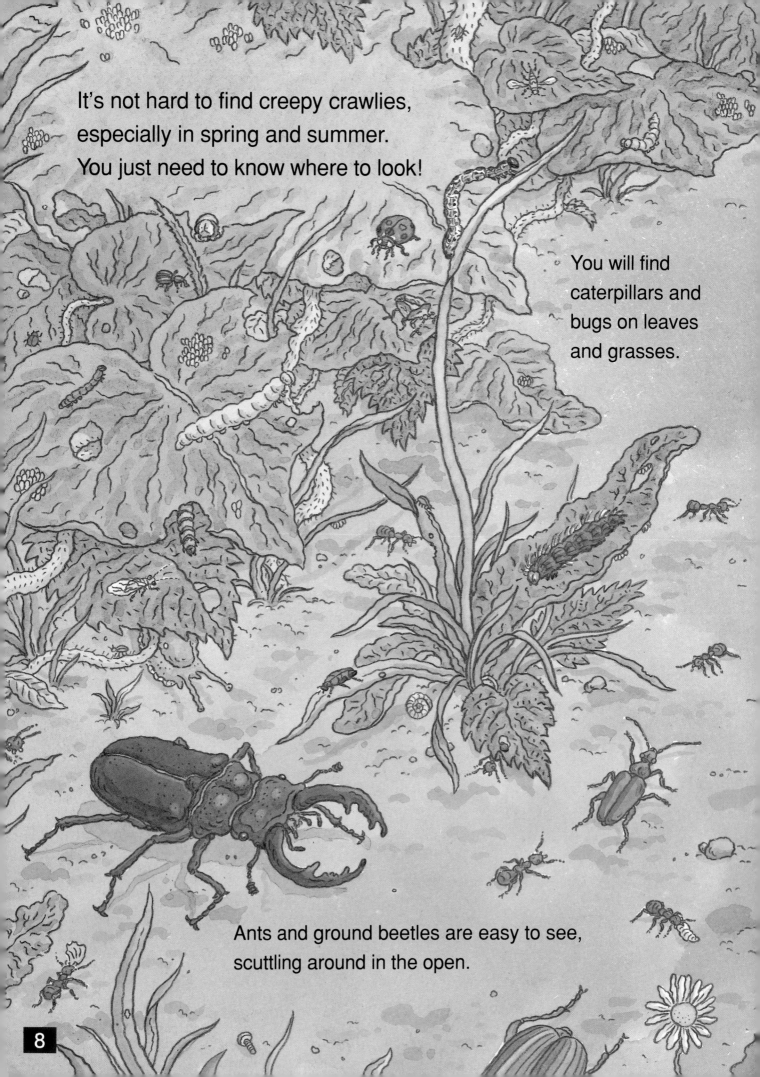

It's not hard to find creepy crawlies,
especially in spring and summer.
You just need to know where to look!

You will find
caterpillars and
bugs on leaves
and grasses.

Ants and ground beetles are easy to see,
scuttling around in the open.

Look for millipedes, centipedes, and woodlice in damp, dark places among fallen leaves or under stones. Don't forget to put stones back where you found them.

Some creepy crawlies live underground. Dig up some soil to see what you can find.

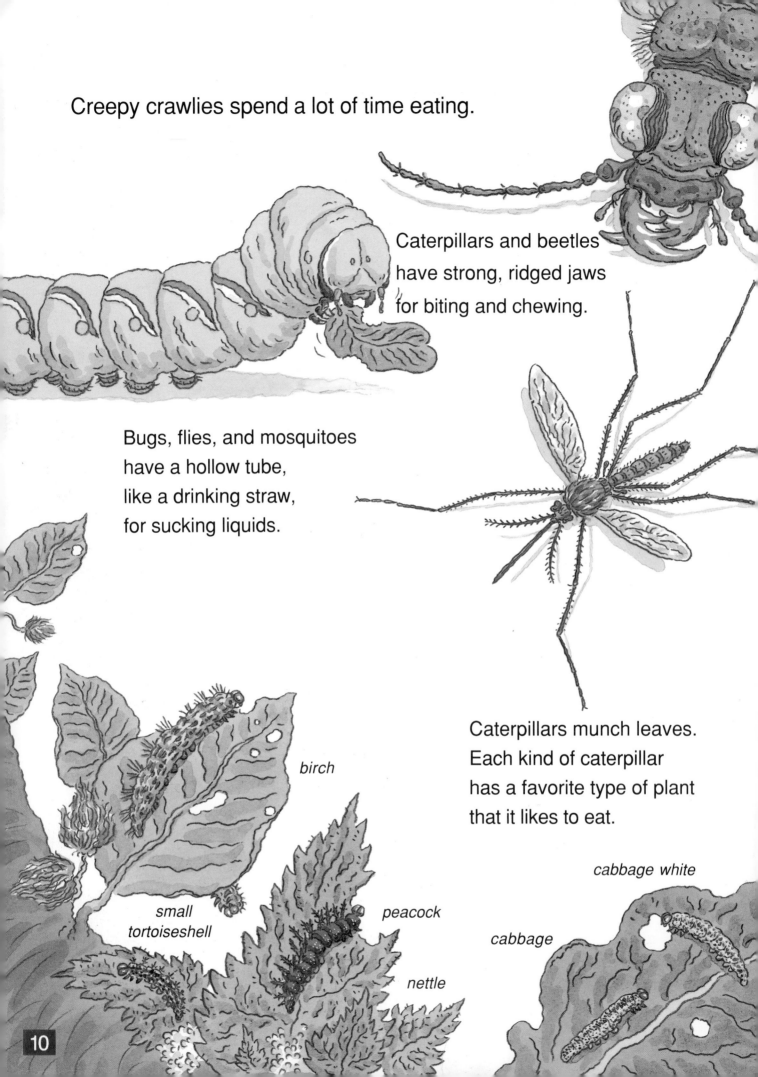

Creepy crawlies spend a lot of time eating.

Caterpillars and beetles
have strong, ridged jaws
for biting and chewing.

Bugs, flies, and mosquitoes
have a hollow tube,
like a drinking straw,
for sucking liquids.

Caterpillars munch leaves.
Each kind of caterpillar
has a favorite type of plant
that it likes to eat.

birch

*small
tortoiseshell*

peacock

nettle

cabbage white

cabbage

These flower beetles eat the pollen inside flowers.

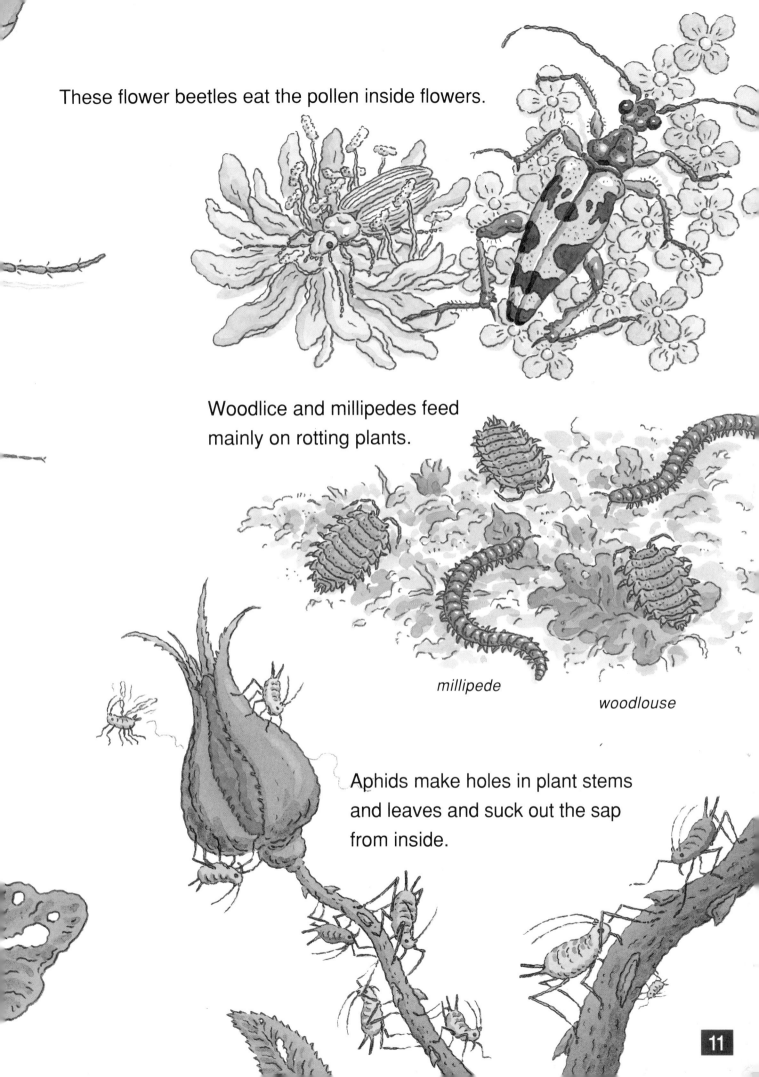

Woodlice and millipedes feed mainly on rotting plants.

millipede

woodlouse

Aphids make holes in plant stems and leaves and suck out the sap from inside.

These creepy crawlies
eat other creepy crawlies.

The assassin bug jabs its sharp mouth
into its prey and sucks the juices inside.

The scorpion seizes insects and spiders
in its big claws and stings them to death
before eating them.

This tiger beetle is very fierce.
It runs fast to catch ants, bugs, and flies
in its strong jaws. It kills its victims
by banging them
on the ground.

This spider has spun a sticky web of silk.
It waits quietly until a juicy fly lands on the web.

When the fly struggles to escape,
the spider poisons it with a bite so it can't move,
and then wraps it in silk. The spider stores the fly
alive in the web until it feels hungry.

Almost all creepy crawlies hatch from eggs. The eggs of ants, beetles, and butterflies hatch into wriggly larvae, which don't look anything like adult insects. Let's see what happens.

These ladybugs are mating.

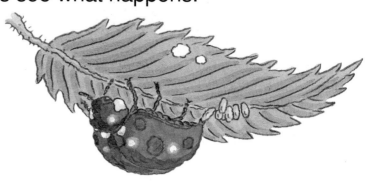

The female lays her eggs on a leaf.

The eggs hatch into tiny larvae.

The larvae eat aphids. They eat and eat and eat. As they eat, they grow.

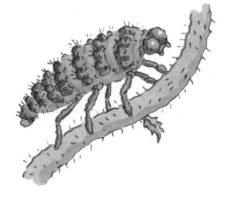

As a larva grows, its skin becomes too tight. A new soft skin grows underneath.

The old skin splits and the larva wriggles and pulls its way out in its new skin. This is called molting.

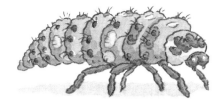

The new skin is soft at first.
The larva can stretch into it.
Later the skin hardens.

It grows very fat. It stops eating.
It stops growing.

Its skin splits one last time
and the larva turns into a pupa.

The ladybug pushes itself
out of the pupa.
Its body is soft and pale.

The larva molts four times.
Orange markings appear
on its body.

It finds a safe place under a leaf
and fixes itself to the stem.

Inside the pupa, an amazing
change takes place. The pupa
turns into a ladybug.

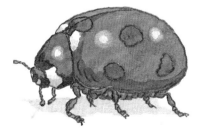

Slowly its body dries.
Its wing cases harden
and its spots appear.

Some creepy crawlies hatch
looking like small adults,
but they don't have wings.
They are called nymphs.

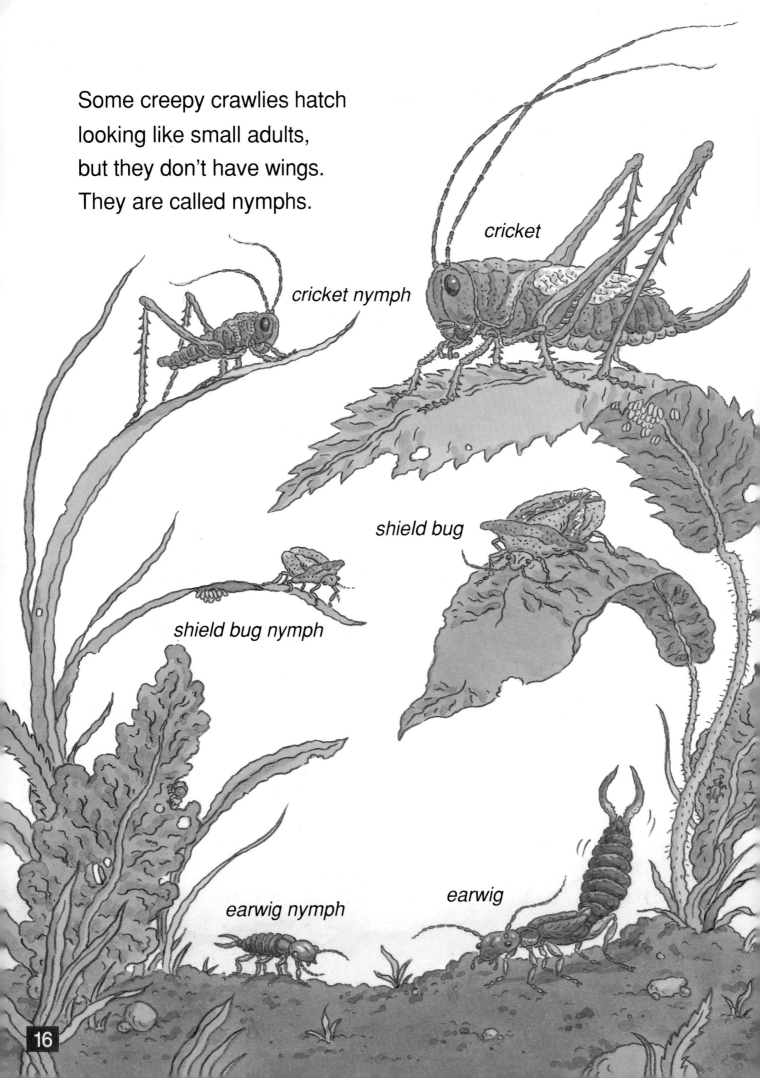

cricket

cricket nymph

shield bug

shield bug nymph

earwig nymph

earwig

A grasshopper nymph molts several times
before it is fully grown. Each time it molts,
it gets bigger . . .

and bigger . . .

and bigger . . .

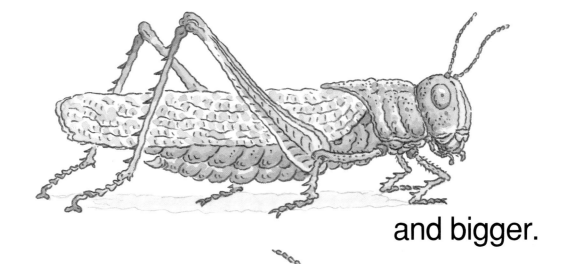

and bigger.

And each time it molts,
its wing buds grow a little more.
At the last molt, the wings are fully grown
and it is an adult. It doesn't grow any more.

Creepy crawlies don't have noses, ears, fingers,
or tongues. Their eyes are quite different from ours.
But they can still smell, hear, touch, taste, and see!

Insects taste and smell with their antennae.
These are the prongs on the front of their heads.
Antennae come in all shapes and sizes.

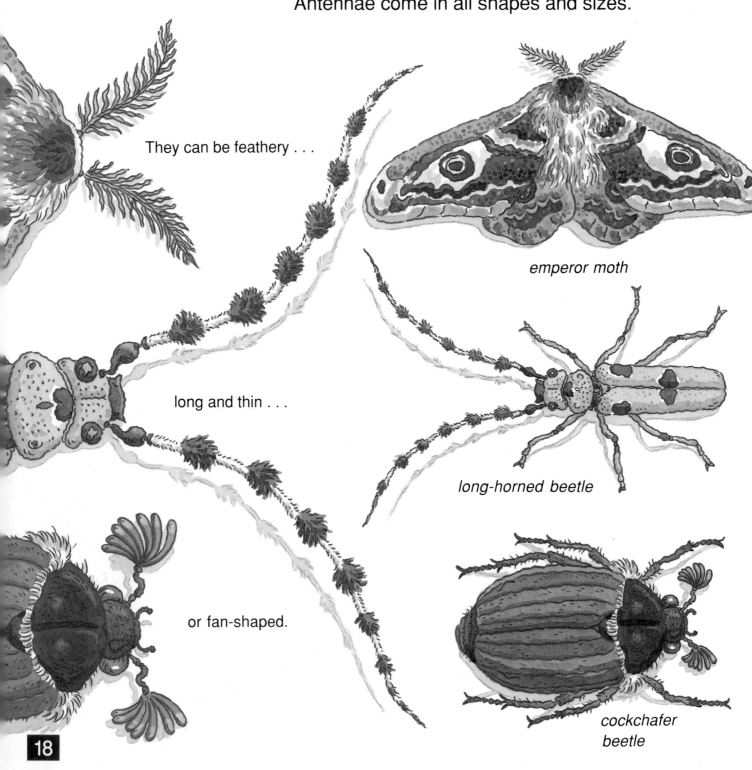

They can be feathery . . .

emperor moth

long and thin . . .

long-horned beetle

or fan-shaped.

cockchafer
beetle

Most insects are covered
with tiny, stiff hairs.
These are sensitive to touch.

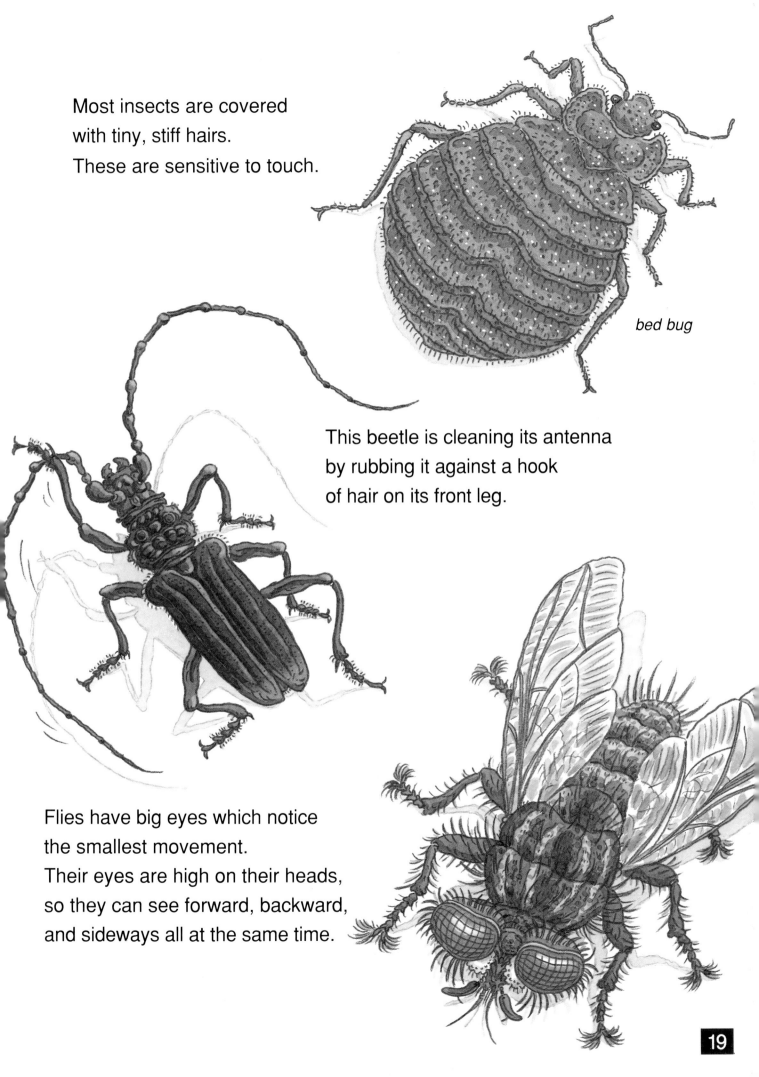

bed bug

This beetle is cleaning its antenna
by rubbing it against a hook
of hair on its front leg.

Flies have big eyes which notice
the smallest movement.
Their eyes are high on their heads,
so they can see forward, backward,
and sideways all at the same time.

One thing you're sure to notice
is that many creepy crawlies are
always on the move.

ladybug

You may be surprised that some beetles can fly.
Under their hard wing cases are wings.
The beetles fold their wings back
under their wing cases when they land.

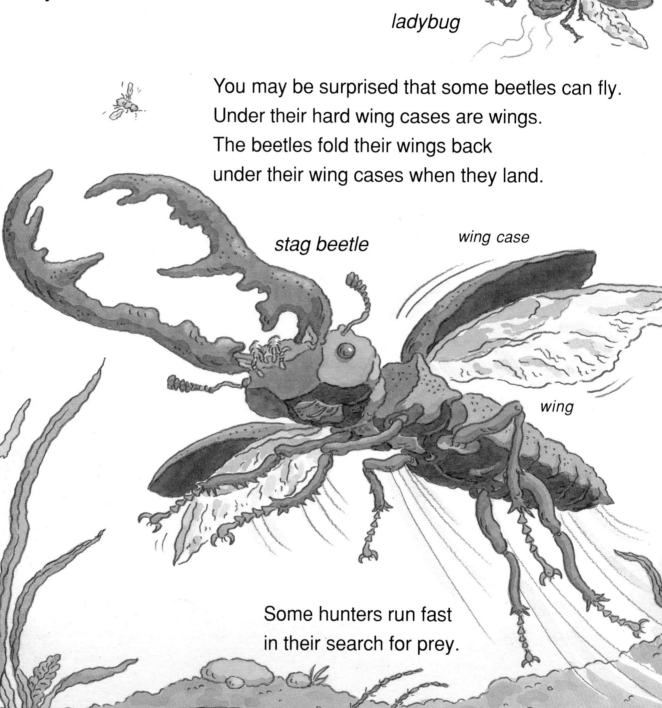

stag beetle

wing case

wing

Some hunters run fast
in their search for prey.

tiger beetle

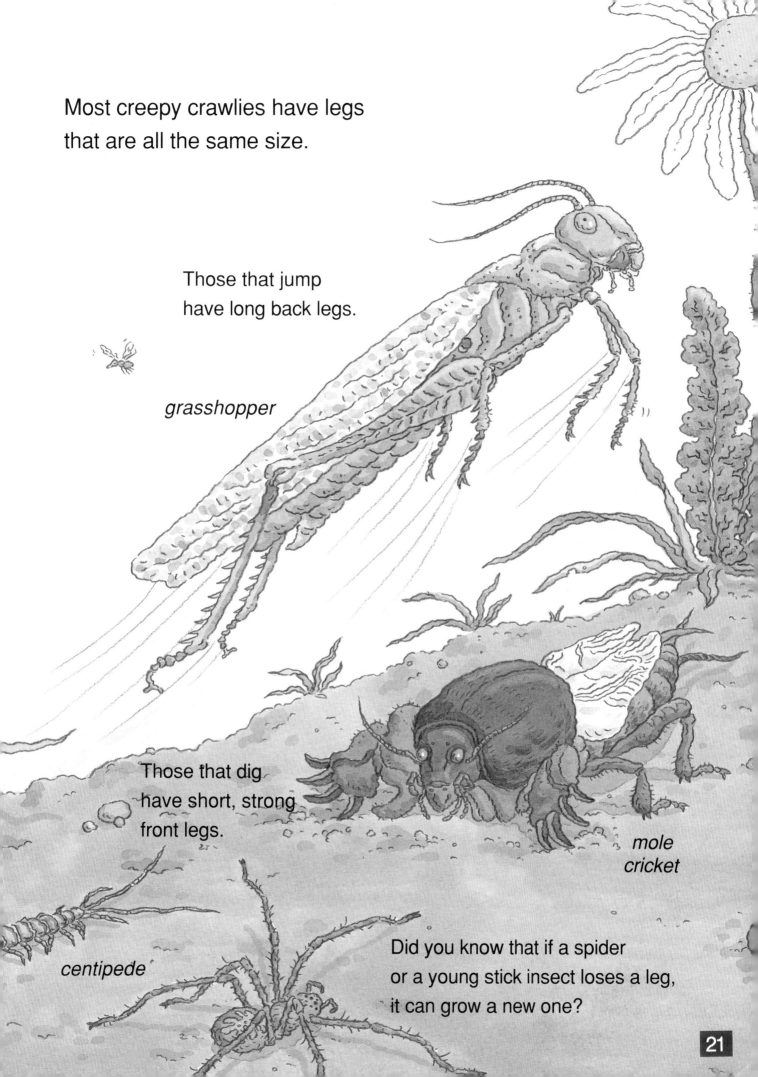

Most creepy crawlies have legs
that are all the same size.

Those that jump
have long back legs.

grasshopper

Those that dig
have short, strong
front legs.

*mole
cricket*

centipede

Did you know that if a spider
or a young stick insect loses a leg,
it can grow a new one?

Creepy crawlies have ways of protecting
themselves against hungry enemies.

Some creepy crawlies are the same color
and shape as their surroundings.
This is called camouflage. Try saying it.
When they keep still, they are hard to spot.
Can you see a stick insect, a caterpillar,
a moth, and a grasshopper hiding
in this picture?

A pill millipede curls
itself into a tight ball
if it is disturbed.

Enemies mainly attack creepy crawlies which move. So in times of danger, they pull in their legs and lie very still. Can you see a spider and a ladybug protecting themselves like this?

Some creepy crawlies can give an enemy a big surprise.

The puss moth caterpillar raises its head and looks frightening.

The bombardier beetle fires out a loud pop and a cloud of poisonous spray.

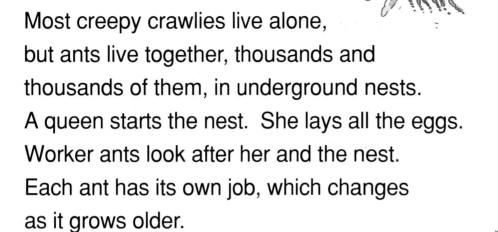

Most creepy crawlies live alone,
but ants live together, thousands and
thousands of them, in underground nests.
A queen starts the nest. She lays all the eggs.
Worker ants look after her and the nest.
Each ant has its own job, which changes
as it grows older.

Ants are good at
finding their way
about. They leave a
scent trail to food for
other ants to follow.

Some workers fetch
twigs and bits of leaf
to mend the nest.
The underground part
is covered with a mound
of twigs which keeps it
warm and dry.

Ants beware!
This lurking beetle
is after you.

Ants love sweet foods.
Aphids make a sugary
juice called honeydew,
which ants like to eat.

Ants clean their nests.
They put garbage
in special chambers
or take it outside the nest.

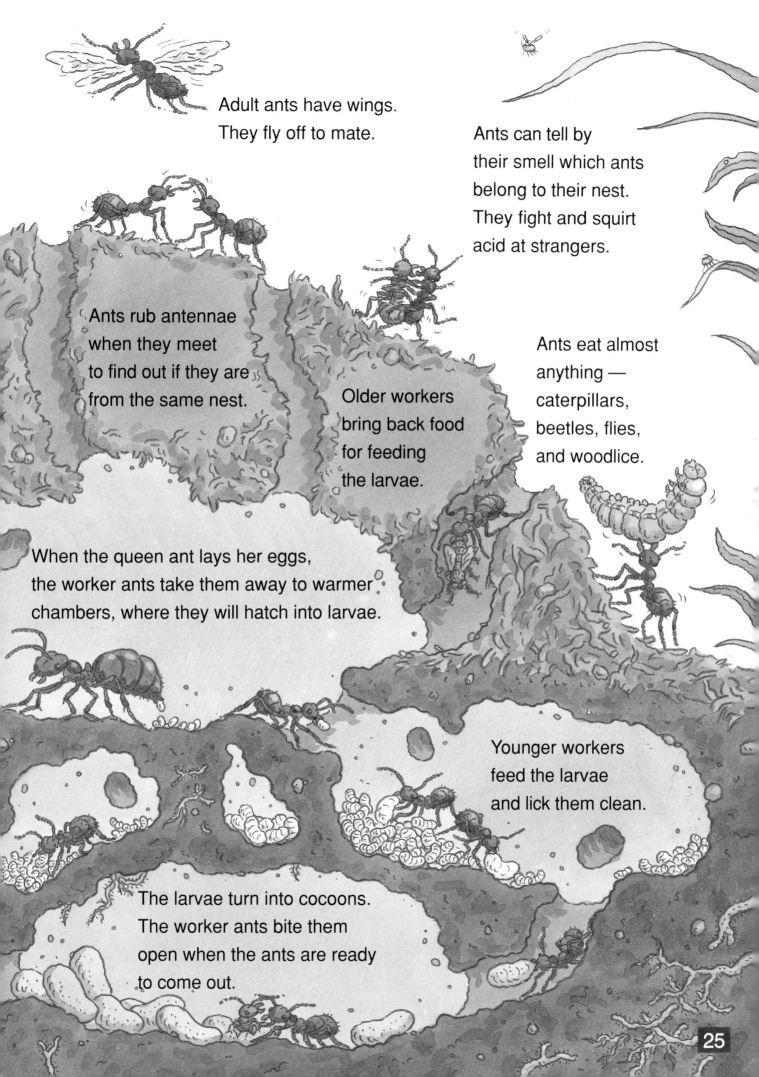

Adult ants have wings.
They fly off to mate.

Ants can tell by
their smell which ants
belong to their nest.
They fight and squirt
acid at strangers.

Ants rub antennae
when they meet
to find out if they are
from the same nest.

Older workers
bring back food
for feeding
the larvae.

Ants eat almost
anything —
caterpillars,
beetles, flies,
and woodlice.

When the queen ant lays her eggs,
the worker ants take them away to warmer
chambers, where they will hatch into larvae.

Younger workers
feed the larvae
and lick them clean.

The larvae turn into cocoons.
The worker ants bite them
open when the ants are ready
to come out.

Some creepy crawlies can be very helpful
to us, while others are pests.
The helpful ones feed on some of the pests,
help improve the soil, and neaten up.
The pests eat farmers' crops, destroy wood,
and pass on diseases.

Can you guess which of these creepy crawlies
are helpers and which are pests?

Lacewings and ladybugs
eat the aphids
which can spoil plants.
Every ladybug eats 30
aphids a day.

The Colorado beetle, which lives
in the United States, attacks
potato crops.

Grain weevils spoil stored grain.
They bore into the seeds
with their snouts and lay eggs
inside. The larvae feed on the grain.

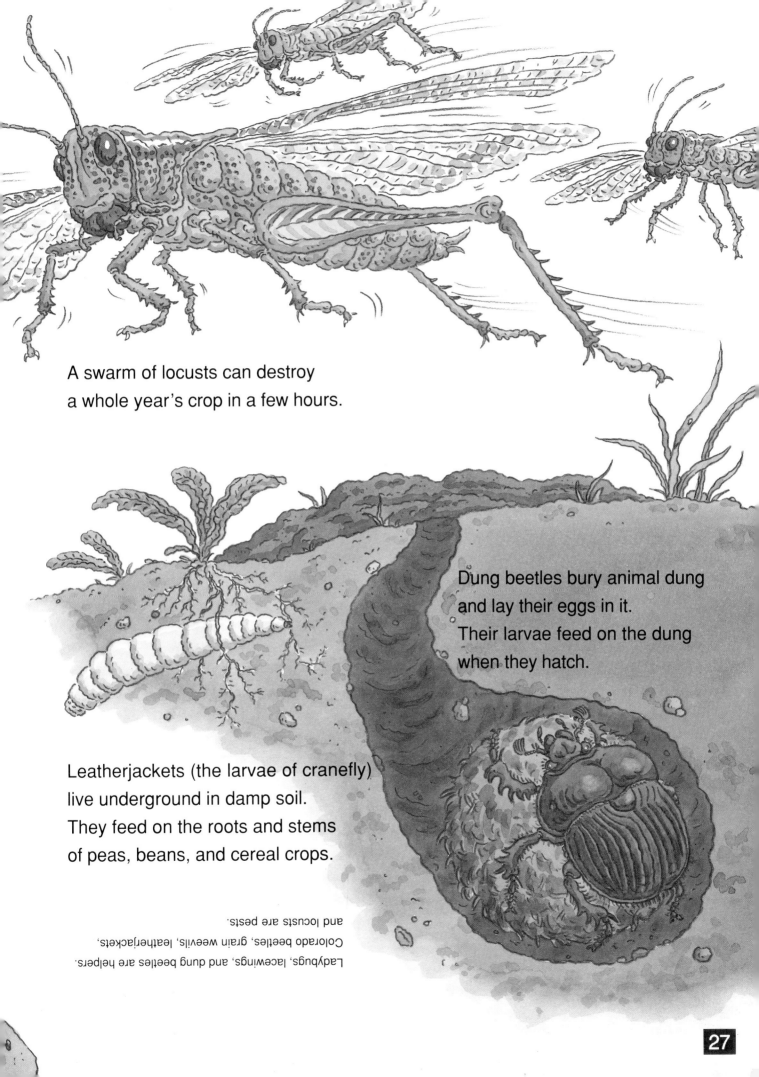

A swarm of locusts can destroy
a whole year's crop in a few hours.

Dung beetles bury animal dung
and lay their eggs in it.
Their larvae feed on the dung
when they hatch.

Leatherjackets (the larvae of cranefly)
live underground in damp soil.
They feed on the roots and stems
of peas, beans, and cereal crops.

Ladybugs, lacewings, and dung beetles are helpers.
Colorado beetles, grain weevils, leatherjackets,
and locusts are pests.

Collect some creepy crawlies
for a little while to have a closer look.
They are very fragile, so don't hold them for long.
Use a soft brush to push them gently into a jar or box.
The best container for creepy crawlies is a fish tank.
Cover it with muslin, or a lid with plenty of holes.

A home for caterpillars

Put a jar in a cool place out
of the sun. Caterpillars need
fresh leaves every day.
Be sure to give them the type
of leaves you found them on.
If you can't, it's best not to keep
caterpillars, because they will die.

A home for millipedes

Line the base of the tank
with damp compost, dead leaves,
rotting wood, twigs, and bark.
Put in a shallow bowl of water with
cotton wool in it. Feed the millipedes
with little bits of raw fruit and
vegetable peelings.

A home for ladybugs

Ladybugs eat aphids, which you will find on many garden plants, especially roses. Cut rose bud shoots and stand them in water to keep them fresh.

A home for a black ground beetle

Only keep *one* beetle at a time.
Line the tank with a deep layer
of damp soil (which you must keep damp).
Put in some large stones and a piece
of rotting wood for the beetle to hide under.
This beetle eats slugs and worms.
You could also give it small pieces
of meat.

A home for grasshoppers

Be warned — grasshoppers are very tricky to catch. Keep them in a covered tank lined with sand or soil. Feed them daily with fresh grass.

Once you have finished looking at creepy crawlies, put them back exactly where you found them or else they may die.

There goes the black ground beetle.

INDEX

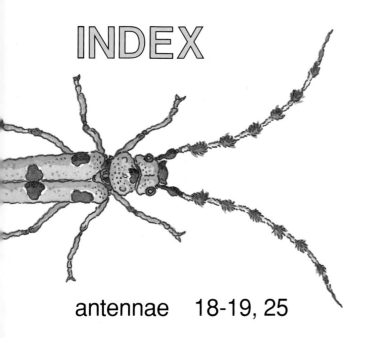

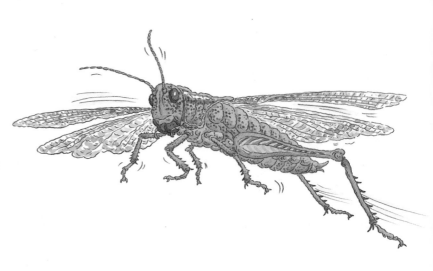

BASICS

An introduction to our world